MONSTER MANNERS

In the Classroom

Written by
Charis Mather

Designed by
Amy Li

In the Classroom © 2024 BookLife Publishing
This edition is published by arrangement with BookLife Publishing

Library of Congress Control Number:
The Library of Congress Control Number is available on the Library of Congress website.

ISBN
979-8-89359-330-3 (library bound)
979-8-89359-414-0 (paperback)
979-8-89359-385-3 (epub)
979-8-89359-360-0 (hosted ebook)

Printed in the United States of America
Mankato, MN
092025

sales@northstareditions.com
888-417-0195

Written by:
Charis Mather

Edited by:
Rebecca Phillips-Bartlett

Designed by:
Amy Li

PHOTO CREDITS
All images are courtesy of Shutterstock.com, unless otherwise specified. With thanks to Getty Images, ThinkStock Photo and iStockphoto.

Cover – mckenna71, Archiwiz, Animado. Recurring – Agafonov Oleg, Omeris. P2–3 – Angelina Bambina. P16–17 – Animado. P19–21 – nik–nadal.

Monsters know many things.

They know how to count and how to measure...

They know how to tell the time and how to read...

But there is one thing that many monsters do not know...

MANNERS!

The playground was noisy with chatter as all the monsters waited for the classroom doors to open. It was the first day of school. Everyone was super excited—and a little nervous.

"I heard that Mr. Monclair has lots of rules," one little monster said.

"I heard that too," said another.

Just then, the doors opened. Some monsters whispered excitedly to each other. Others cheered. Mr. Monclair stepped out and clapped his hands to ask for quiet.

"Good morning, students!" he said. "Welcome to my class. You might have heard that I have a lot of classroom rules. Well, the truth is that I only have one big rule: please mind your manners!"

"There are lots of ways to show your manners," Mr. Monclair said. "One of them is to line up before coming into the classroom. Do you think you could do that for me?"

"Yes, Mr. Monclair!" the monsters said. They all lined up by the doors.

"Wonderful," said Mr. Monclair, waving his hand for them to go inside. "Please find your desks. We have many more monster manners to learn."

The students filed in. They each found the desk with their name.

Mr. Monclair came to the front of the class. "You all did such a good job at lining up that I think you are ready to learn another monster manner. Are you listening carefully?" he asked.

"Yes, Mr. Monclair!" they said.

"Monsters with good manners show me that they are paying attention when I speak," Mr. Monclair said. "How can you show me that?"

"We can sit still!" one monster said.

"We can stay quiet while you are talking!" said another.

"We can look at you instead of each other!" said a third.

"Yes, yes, and yes," said Mr. Monclair. "Those are great answers. All of those things show me that you are ready to listen. Sitting still and not shouting out or looking around at your friends can be hard. But doing these things will help you not get distracted while you learn."

"If you have something to say or a question to ask, you can put your hand up and wait for me to say your name," Mr. Monclair added.

Right away, Stomp's hand shot up. He had a frown on his face.

"Yes, Stomp?" Mr. Monclair said.

"Those things sound really hard to do," Stomp said. "I love learning, but I also love shouting and stomping. And I have so many eyes that all want to look at different things all the time!"

Mr. Monclair nodded in understanding. "Sometimes having good manners is hard—especially for little monsters!"

Mr. Monclair pulled open a drawer in his desk. He grabbed something for Stomp.

"This is a fidget. It can help you focus when your eyes are distracted and your body wants to wiggle. Use this fidget to help you listen in class. Save your stomping and shouting for break time."

"Thanks, Mr. Monclair!" said Stomp.

Mr. Monclair turned to the class. "Can anyone tell me why monsters with good manners shouldn't shout in class?"

Dot put her hand up high. "If we all shout, no one will be able to hear anyone," she said.

"That's right, Dot," said Mr. Monclair. "We should help each other make the classroom the best place possible for learning." Mr. Monclair began handing out workbooks. "Let's practice being calm and quiet now. When everyone is done with their work, we can have our break time."

The little monsters started working quietly. Some monsters finished early.

Addy got hungry and started chewing her pencils.

Dot got bored and started doodling on her workbook—and then on the desk.

Tickles found a loose screw in her desk. She put it in her pocket to take home and show her dad.

Patch started tearing out little pieces of paper.

When Mr. Monclair came around to collect the workbooks, he noticed the doodles, the chewed pencils, the torn-up paper, and the missing screw.

"Oh dear," he said. "That won't do. I think it's time for another lesson about monster manners."

"Monsters with good manners look after their classroom supplies. That means not drawing on things or breaking things. We want our classroom to stay nice and clean, don't we?"

"Yes!" agreed the monsters.

"Let's work together to clean up," said Mr. Monclair.

As the monsters were tidying up the bits of torn paper, Mr. Monclair suddenly had an itch in his nose.

As the sneeze grew, Mr. Monclair threw his elbow in front of his mouth and nose.

"True," said Mr. Monclair. "Using your elbow or a tissue is the best way to catch a sneeze. This stops germs going everywhere. Monsters with good manners catch their coughs and sneezes so the classroom stays clean."

Soon, the classroom was clean again. The students went back to their seats. Mr. Monclair looked around. They were all sitting still. He had a big smile on his face.

"Who would have thought that you little monsters could learn so many manners in one morning! You should all be very proud of yourselves."

Stomp put his hand up.

"Yes, Stomp?" said Mr. Monclair.

"Does that mean it is break time now?" he asked.

Mr. Monclair grinned and opened
the door to the playground.
"Yes, it does!"

The class let out a big cheer.

Not all monsters have good manners, but Mr. Monclair's students do. Do you?

Can you remember Mr. Monclair's classroom manners?

- Line up neatly before going into class.
- Pay attention to the teacher.
- Don't shout out in class.
- Take care of the classroom supplies.
- Catch your coughs and sneezes to keep the classroom clean.

MONSTER manners

Young monsters may not be known for their manners, but they are always excited to learn new things. Can Mr. Monclair's new class learn to mind their manners in the classroom?

Titles in this series:

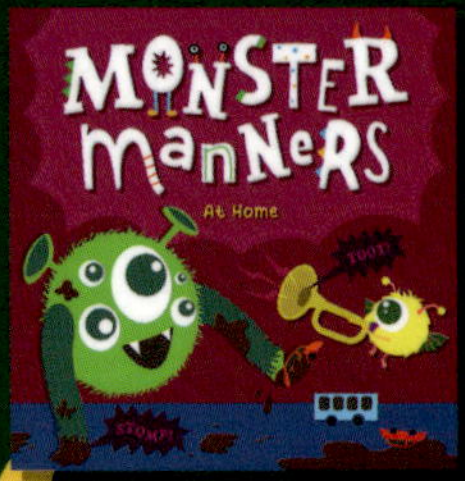

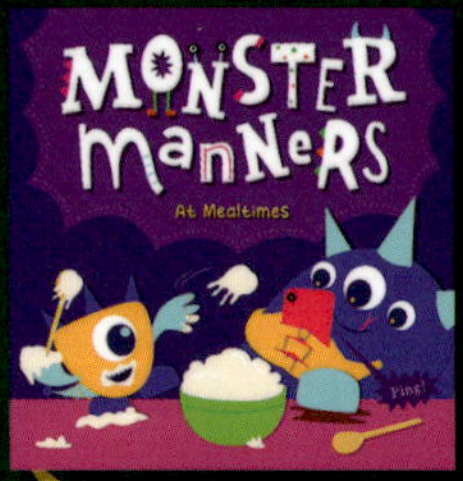

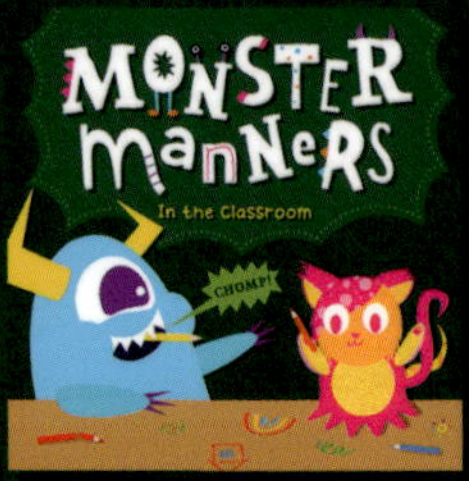

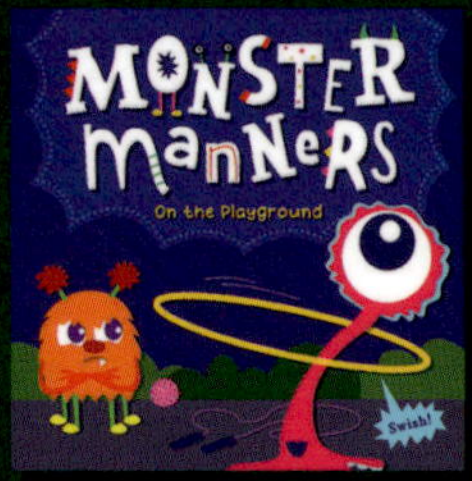

maple bay

ISBN: 979-8-89359-414-0
90000
9 798893 594140

Deer

From Head to Hoof

Alex Hall